The Year of God and Other Poems

Subramaniam Cheemalapati

 pencil

ISBN 978-93-5610-193-7
© Subramaniam Cheemalapati 2022
Published in India 2022 by Pencil

A brand of
One Point Six Technologies Pvt. Ltd.
123, Building J2, Shram Seva Premises,
Wadala Truck Terminal, Wadala (E)
Mumbai 400037, Maharashtra, INDIA
E connect@thepencilapp.com
W www.thepencilapp.com

DISCLAIMER: *The opinions expressed in this book are those of the authors and do not purport to reflect the views of the Publisher.*

Author biography

Subramaniam Cheemalapati writes poetry, short stories, essays, and fiction.

THE YEAR OF GOD AND OTHER POEMS is his first book of poems. He is currently working on another poetry book and a thriller novel.

He lives in Bangalore with his family.

Before starting writing, Subramaniam is an engineering and management graduate. After that, just to shake things up, he started his career as a programmer, and risen through the career graph. He loves to read poetry, literary fiction, and non-fiction. He is now back to his favorite passion – writing.

CONTENTS

Epigraph

"You've made it through. Give thyself a poem."

Acknowledgements

First and foremost, I would like to thank God for giving me humility, mental peace, strength, ideas, and motivation to ride through the toughest phase of the pandemic. It has been very difficult times.

To my dear wife Seetha and my sons Santhosh and Shashank, for riding the pandemic together looking positively, and mutual support.

Life's truly unpredictable.

DAY 1 22-MAR-2020, MYSORE, INDIA

There's life. There's this Covid-19. Life is prevalent since ages. Covid-19 is spreading pages. It is a chain. Like the financial scams we have seen. One man infecting many. Those infected gathering more followers, and so on. Until the chain of infection breaks. So rare. Then we see wickets fall. People die. This is the logic. This is the pattern. Then there are measures. Facing a pandemic with certain boldness.

The lockdown begins.

The world was full of life. Yes, there were disturbances between countries. Not meltdowns within individual countries. Until we saw it play out in front of us. Wuhan came. The world reacted. India too. Infections grew. Lockdown, quarantine words became a reality. On a scale we have never seen before.

Quarantine.

It was never a bad thing to be locked inside the house, talking only to the walls, corners, and furniture. It has become quieter, quieter.

It was never like this before.

For the first time, I obeyed an instruction which I could never ever do – stay put in one place, within wider inert walls, for days. I would sit on my table, and peer into my laptop, and see what the world around me was like. What was happening. What happened to those who ventured out. Who all got spanked, who all did monkey pushups? It was a like a drone view, trying to imagine what was happening, what I missed.

Janata Curfew, Sunday 22nd March 2020.

The curfew by the people, of the people, for the people. A.k.a People's Curfew. The democratic India celebrates a curfew. Sometimes in the evening, I heard banging of utensils, and claps. What I saw was a celebration of togetherness against an unknown, unseen enemy. Women standing in the middle of the garden, singing opera style, while many stood in their balconies clapping hands, utensils, and banging on anything which makes sound.

Entire India tries to stay united, like a fist.

I always cared about life. Everyone is entitled to live their life to the fullest. It is a critical time, and India is no stranger to pandemics.

Plague, Spanish Fever come to mind, with millions of deaths. There are articles in newspapers of how India faced the bubonic plague of 1890s. How the pandemic entered Bangalore, and how it spread to all the areas around the city. The idea is getting a sense of pandemic then versus the pandemic now, makes us feel positive. Again, every disease brings out the same old, time-tested fear. The sick fills the nursing clinics.

Then the body bags.

There's always a fear striking us: How will the virus enter my home? Every time, the people went through existential consequences. Some survived, many perished. Then several years of lull, before other strikes again. Same methodology, different virus. The population is ravaged. What do we really learn for our own future? For the future generations not to face the same fate. I doubt humans have that far-fetched thinking. Especially with our leaders focused on immediate political future.

I wish I had more insight as to how the virus is working, once inside. I am looking. Trying to find research, to understand the pathogen's behavior. What does it look like? I am deep into the world-wide-web. There is so much out there. It is late into the night. 2AM to be exact. I am worried. I am anxious. I look at my wife, and children deep asleep. There is a deep desire to know the virus and execute ways to defeat it. And of course, I have Wuhan — available for free.

REPAIR

The day just passed by

and all that's seen of clock

are non-movable hands, tied at hinges,

right-angled, frozen

like ice glaciers, arctic

igloos with room only for shelter.

I tried to get it repaired,

A new battery to power

of which we are made,

another new screen,

replacing the broken one.

What did I do?

My time was bad.

I threw the watch on the wall.

A dent appeared, amidst

weight of broken dreams.

Do you not see?

Or care for me?

Subdued, insulted,

Buried in lost time,

In lost career.

My time was bad.

I threw the watch on the wall, again,

Broken, strewn, pieces

reflect a life thrown,

left to fend a disable

child, harping to survive.

IMMUNITY

The great war has not ended, deaths coming

in numbers to see, covering fear seeping in –

will I be the next? Will I bring to my home?

You have no answers, the questions

you took with bright smiles and forceful hand,

you know the answers are available in guides,

newspapers, and television, all over internet.

The world has them already, spidery thoughts lining

the paths to heaven. I don't want to die; I hear your sobs.

Can't you see it coming, like an all-pervasive ghost

Out to scare you to death. I hear your sobs. I hear mine too.

What sets it apart, your own immunity, your inner strength,

Don't worry, hear me out, hear the saints, hear the positivity,

hear all natural, hear yourself, thy will heal with immunity!

DAY 36 29-APR-2020, MYSORE, INDIA

An Icon No More

Moon plays hide and seek with us.

Stars don't.

RIP Irrfan Khan.

You are a star.

DAY 37 30-APR-2020, MYSORE, INDIA

Another Icon No More

Moon plays hide and seek with us.

Stars don't.

RIP Rishi Kapoor.

You are another star.

DAY 44 7-MAY-2020, MYSORE, INDIA

The Gas Tragedy

From one tragedy to another. India is in for a bumpy ride throughout this Covid-19 crisis. I woke up to a heart wrenching video. Whatsapp video sharing is rampant.

I ignored the video as usual.

I was observing the funerals of the two film stalwarts who died in the last 2 days of April 2020.

Gas leak struck in Vishakapatnam.

Hundreds fell like pins.

Just like that.

THE REAL FRIEND

Look no further, don't go out,

for the corona virus is almost

in us, wherever you look for it,

in the community

in and out of our society,

for we can't see, our

symptoms are pointer

to what the virus can

stitch it all for us

front and back, no fruits.

Our warriors fear it, for

it can kill, maim, and infect

all their family, and we

as a society are scared too

to get infected and reinfection all.

There are no friends, who can

drive the fear our of us, drive

sense into our sickening mind.

our warriors are dying, with virus,

with guilt of inviting the virus.

There are no friends, my friend, who

let us see the fragility of life, what the world

outside virus can be, it is the same

as what we all seek, peace, happy,

life overflowing in solace.

DAY 54 17-MAY-2020, MYSORE, INDIA

Zombie Town

Mysuru is out of woods.

Or so, it seemed. A function was organized yesterday to reward and felicitate the Corona Warriors. The curve is flattened. The number of cases reduced to zero. All patients saved and alive.

Still, when I went out today afternoon. I felt scared, as if I was in a zombie town. The streets were almost empty. Compared to normal Sundays, I see almost 90% less. Several scooter riders with three passengers zipped fast, as I drove slowly. There was an old man sitting on the side, with his mangoes spread over a cloth. Each face clearly was not happy. I wanted to stop by, try to probe into the man's mind. What was the man thinking?

For a minute, I felt scared. The Corona virus cases were increasing in India, and several adjoining states have their numbers rising exponentially. With thousands of migrants ready to travel into Mysuru, the zero-case scenario might not last. Also, the next district (Mandya) has positive cases rising into twenties per day. I felt a sudden chill, as if the city turned into ghost city.

Can we ever go back to the way of life we were used to before? Will we get infected by this dreaded Corona virus? Why is this virus so deadly? There is no cure nor vaccine until today. Why do all viruses emanate from China?

I don't have the answers.

DAY 55 18-MAY-2020, MYSORE, INDIA

Zombie Dreams

I am writing this, early in the morning. 4am to be precise. I couldn't sleep throughout the night.

Perhaps, I was afraid, or scared of the future.

DAY 61 24-MAY-2020, MYSORE, INDIA

New York Times

It is New York Times day.

I woke up with headlines on the iconic New York Times. A full front page of names, as US neared 1 lakh deaths. An incredible feat. I was overwhelmed as I read the uniqueness behind the lives lost. Silent tears rolled in me.

There is death all around here, in my country too. Older patients are becoming positive in larger numbers. Who knows we might see some causalities in them? The elders I have known for several years. Are afraid to even step out of their houses. They are doing all housework themselves, without allowing even house helps into their homes. The continuous lockdown is making them crazy too. They are craving for their loved ones to come – wherever they are now. Many times, the elders are threatening their loved ones not to handover their property post their demise. It is catch-22 for the loved ones. They would not like to be the virus carrier into their parents/elders' homes. So much uncertainty this pandemic has brought to us. Think about it. How would elders face when they come to know they are infected? Some of them will still be in their bubble, "nothing will happen to me," while others will just panic, with extreme anxiety.

Amid all this pandemic uncertainty, there's one country marching as if on steroids.

China.

Chinese soldiers are flexing in border areas of Ladakh. Indian soldiers seem to match them at least it is appearing to be so. And China seem to take over Hong Kong.

Finally.

Chinese always had a way to do things surreptitiously. Slithering like a snake into the midst, surprising us – almost shocking us. This COVID-19 pandemic is no different. There's a silent fear growing among all of us that this was Chinese way of getting back at the world. I wish all this is not true, just some hunch.

Lockdown 4.0 is still ongoing. Next week might be last. The lockdown is really hurting my mind. I feel I am becoming mentally sick. I seem to talk to my shadows, talking to my other self in the mirror. At times, I feel hollow, unable to express myself. I don't want to show my baser side to my family.

I am a good guy, mentally sick.

MAMA'S BOY

I

Thousands assembled at the railway station,

social distancing? What distancing?

each body, touching other, bouncing

between hope and despair;

there's a method to madness

of what corona virus lockdowns

can do for all people embedded,

men, women, and migrants

rushed out of where they live

like a plucked fruit, cut, and spread

like a salad, sprinkled with garam masala –

some went as far as the two legs can take them,

some went as far as their lives can take them,

survival, deaths with those they care.

II

The bedsheet covering half-body, head resting

concrete floor on the railway platform, the view

is scattered to the luggage, two bags

placed near the platform support, a playful

boy, tugging at the shroud, the body in eternal sleep,

after days of journey, not knowing, the boy tries,

looking around, as if asking, "can you wake my mamma?"

the words damaged, no sobs, trying to wake,

nature's wooden logs, lying motionless,

our greatest weakness, inability to bring

to life, to sway a mother to her son's wails,

until the world sees what happened,

o boy, o mother, you woke us all,

as a species to see beyond, flawed to truth.

NOTES: PATNA: In one of the most heart-rending visuals of the migrant crisis triggered by the Covid-mandated lockdown, a viral video showed a toddler trying to wake up his dead mother at the railway platform in Muzaffarpur, Bihar. The child is seen pulling up a sheet of cloth covering his mother's body in an attempt to wake her up. The woman, 35-year-old Avreena Khatoon, died on board the Ahmedabad-Katihar (Bihar) Shramik Special train, on Monday. The body was kept on the platform till an ambulance arrived to take it to her home in Katihar district. The video shows the child walking up to his mother's body, tugging at the sheet placed over and covering himself with it. "This small child doesn't know that the bedsheet with which he is playing is the shroud of his mother who has gone into eternal sleep. This mother

died of hunger and thirst after being on a train for four
days.

III

Migrant, don't cry on the roadside.

You can travel now, the lockdown is not

against you. It is for you.

Don't cry, migrant.

Lockdown has made you weak, with no work,

no money, you made the Nizamuddin Bridge

your home, your phone, your son

died, and you were not there.

You wept, your wife and daughter in Bihar cried too.

Don't cry, my friend. I promise you will find a way.

God is kind too. He was there, with money

And car to get you to the Delhi railway station,

Shramik Special train waiting for you

with a paid ticket. Don't cry migrant.

Yes, you need to return, by right,

No one can stop you, also, no one

Can stop the corona virus too.

So quarantine. Whine your time,

before your blood-relative come to you,

don't you mistake the fate; it has been kind to you,

while it let many die several deaths.

28

IV Royals

The thick woody trunk grew over a wide area,

O banyan tree, your roots are your expanse.

You grow, provide shelter, vast like a mother's bosom,

forever sense of safety, when I am with you.

You are my go-to, your acts I follow, ideal,

instinct-driven, unlike a hollow trunk.

No doubt you are the royals of the country,

for your generations and mine too.

Then this corona virus, sneaking into our body,

harm or no harm, bodies having money or not,

saving only those who are honest and submissive

or the grateful becoming of our fear, let alone

unforgiving those with money, and royalties.

O banyan tree! O royals! You are too, in the clutch!

DAY 63 26-MAY-2020, MYSORE, INDIA

China and Pandemic

'Prepare for war': China's Xi Jinping tells his army.

Such is the mindset in a lifetime pandemic situation. People are falling sick in large numbers and dying of Covid-19. All over the world, countries are overwhelmed by the rising pandemic. The strategies to control the pandemic is producing mixed results. In India the situation has changed since the low numbers of lockdowns. The cases are rising. In this situation, Chinese soldiers are trying to bulldoze India into a war. There are war games on the Ladakh region border. Entire India is gauging Chinese mood for a war, and eager to see the Indian response. We lost one war earlier. The Chinese are ruthless soldiers. But this is not the time for a war. This is life and death for millions as the corona virus is spreading all around. Whatever happened to Chinese sensibilities. There is a saying, a knife only can cut a knife. It is time for the world to join and face China.

Perhaps this is the Fourth World War. World versus China. And another N-bomb.

Let's see how the events pan out as we move months.

DAY 64 27-MAY-2020, MYSORE, INDIA

Mumbai Deaths, US Deaths

"Till death separates us apart"

Maharashtra Corona Virus deaths spiked above 100 for the first time. Mumbai is famous for its slums. Remember Slumdog Millionaire?

It is a grim milestone, as more and more deaths are in the offing. Adding to the existing positive cases, we have people moving across states and countries, coming into India. It is almost like ready-made positive cases landing right into the neighborhood.

For me the day wasn't anywhere closer to normal. I argued with my wife. I argued, shouted and went out for 2 hours, trying to keep calm, and my sanity. The rest of the day and night, I kept my mouth shut.

*

100000+ deaths in US.

The number of deaths is difficult to fathom. How could so many deaths in 2-3 months? One death is a missing person. A vacuum which cannot be filled anymore. One hundred thousand is a huge number. A population, a city, a small country. A chill shiver enveloped me. It was time to sleep. More than corona virus, I am dreading the lockdown.

I might lose my sanity, and my family too.

DAY 67 30-MAY-2020, MYSORE, INDIA

I

I woke up suddenly with a jerk, early in the morning. Outside was still dark. I looked at the mini forest covering the Mysore Steel factory premises. I could not but think of the rising corona virus cases in India. The previous day saw rising cases all over the country. Karnataka too saw double century cases. It is community now. I am only worried how close it will come to my family. My family is sleeping. All of us are ready to fight the virus. Because I ordered Fab India Immunity tablets. Like some assurance, just incase.

Positivity.

Positivity begets positive outlook, strong mind, and ability to stay focused.

I looked at my mobile for the time. It was 4.30am.

There's a problem with my country. People still think getting Corona Virus is like a stigma. We are afraid to reveal the cause of death of our elders. We beat up the corona warriors – like doctors, ASHA workers (Accredited Social Health Activists), nurses, and even policemen who try to take people with symptoms for testing, or to move associated to quarantine. I doubt the country will learn in my lifetime. Our superstitions are deep-rooted.

Thousands of people are travelling all over India and coming from foreign countries. All of them need to be tested, and quarantined. I am afraid the numbers will explode if we let these returnees merge with the population.

II

There is lot of anger in US. Looks like George Floyd's death triggered outpouring never seen before in recent times. I am reading CNN and watching videos. The outrage is very destructive. The videos seem jarring to see, with all the destruction happening to the best country in the world. We need effective leadership.

I always followed art, and theatre. Mysuru's Rangayana is still surviving the art in the pandemic. They are using the time to reorganize and restructure their repertoire. I am looking forward to enjoying the works, as soon as possible.

I met the grocery shop owner in Brindavan Gardens. He was so much excited to see me, we talked and talked. He took time to prepare bill for the products purchased by me. We talked about how the corona virus is spreading all over and cases rising. He was so much happy that he reduced Rs. 50 off my bill. He is a perfect gentleman. I liked going to his shop.

DAY 68 31-MAY-2020, MYSORE, INDIA

Unlocking India

There is lot of anger in US. Looks like George Floyd's death triggered outpouring never seen before in recent times. I am reading CNN and watching videos. The outrage is very destructive. The videos seem jarring to see, with all the destruction happening to the best country in the world. We need effective leadership.

I always followed art, and theatre. Mysuru's Rangayana is still surviving the art in the pandemic. They are using the time to reorganize and restructure their repertoire. I am looking forward to enjoying the works, as soon as possible.

I met the grocery shop owner in Brindavan Gardens. He was so much excited to see me, we talked and talked. He took time to prepare bill for the products purchased by me. We talked about how the corona virus is spreading all over and cases rising. He was so much happy that he reduced Rs. 50 off my bill. He is a perfect gentleman. I liked going to his shop.

Indians are known to disinfect our migrants. We spray disinfectant on them. This is a ridiculous practice. The first time it happened in North India in April, I felt nauseated. Since then, it is happening more times. No body seems to bother, especially Health Department of State or Central Government.

Today was supposed to be a full Sunday lockdown, the last full day before fresh guidelines from tomorrow. But yesterday late afternoon, it was announced by Karnataka State Government to allow for no lockdown between 7am and 7pm.

And from tomorrow, we are getting into Unlock# 1. After 4 lockdowns, we will see opening of society in phases. Schools will be closed, though. I went through the unlock#1 guidelines, and also the state guidelines on what's open and what's not.

UNLOCK1 ON AN EMPTY STREET

That day I left

my apartment,

expecting a world outside,

men, women, children,

poor, rich, all cars

reliving the lost days.

What do you see?

Empty streets echo

a zombie town,

reflecting the fear

of corona virus

imploring you to stay put

leave your body and mind

wherever it is, locked

in a virtual world, makeshift

set pieces of everyday

living, pulling you into

it's tighter embrace,

a slight shiver, mindful

of the unknown, unseen,

undefined aspect imploring.

DAY 69 01-JUNE-2020, MYSORE, INDIA

Unlock1 & Wajid

Never thought I will see this – music composer Wajid Khan died of Corona Virus today.

Looks like, he got admitted for Kidney infection, and subsequently throat infection. Then ventilator, and death due to cardiac arrest. Probably kidney ailments lower immunity for covid-19 to attack rapidly when exposed.

I didn't step out of house today. Applied few jobs on portals. I am on leave this week from work.

And spend time arguing with my wife.

DAY 70 02-JUNE-2020, MYSORE, INDIA

An Abnormal Day

Right from the time I woke up, nothing seems to be right. First things first. I slipped and fell in the bathroom in the morning. Since then left ankle pain. This coupled with headache, the day was far from over.

Then I argued with my wife and rushed out – just for a break. Otherwise the arguments, and fights will rise exponentially. Normally, I drive down to a nearby MORE supermarket, park outside at a distance, and spend some time waiting in my car. This is a good diversion.

There are two worries enveloping me. Family issues aside. Corona virus cases, and protests in America. I love America. The best country in the world must not suffer an insult.

Udupi, a temple town, saw 73 cases jump in a single day. And by end of the day today the cases jumped by another 150. The cases are rising all over the state.

43

DAY 75 06-JUNE-2020, MYSORE, INDIA

Welcome Change

Late into the early hours, I saw the adventure movie, SPIDERMAN 4. Then it was Hindi movie NEWTON. It has been quite some time since (decades) I saw movies back 2 back.

What a thrill it was. I couldn't sleep after that.

Then morning came suddenly. I woke up and made coffee. Then bath for my elder son. Santhosh cannot walk. So he needed all the help for a bath; a quick 45 minutes bath.

Then I saw I.T. and I.T. 2. Then I saw Tom Hanks movie THE TERMINAL. Then few videos on the drive to Ladakh. I wanted to see the terrain of India and China fight in Ladakh.

India need to defeat China. If a war erupts, I will join Indian Army.

There is very little I could get out of my mind today. It was highly depressed, and unwilling to even see what lies ahead.

Corona Virus cases in India continued to rise and rose again.

I wound up the day with VEER ZAARA movie. This was a weepie favorite for me.

I put on my blanket and wept to my heart's content.

Silently.

DAY 84 16-JUNE-2020, MYSORE, INDIA

China Kills

The day was shocking. Overnight there was a war on the Eastern Ladakh's Galwan Valley. Chinese soldiers kills scores of Indian soldiers in a surprise attack, then talks of peace were ongoing. Some say, Chinese stabbed India in the back, like a traitor.

Who gets idea to start wars in the time of pandemic, when there is no reason to start itself? Just like a thief, who enters the house next door, and steals to own someone's property, Chinese have used the pandemic garb to steal other countries land, or sovereignty on seas etc. They started a war-like situation, and started to kill our soldiers, mercilessly, with clubs, chains, logs with nails in them, all sort of inhuman way of killings.

All along I thought Chinese were gentlemen nature. They are worse than barbaric, if at all there was a word.

I have started to hate Chinese. I normally don't hate anyone. But Chinese, only.

I couldn't sleep the whole night, browsing websites, to see how all this happened.

Three things torturing my mind – Corona virus, lockdown, loss of jobs, and now Chinese aggression on india border.

My great Himalayas of my dear 73-year old country, soaked in religious hymns, pujas for salvaging, has seen blood. The Galwan river is soaked red, with dead bodies floating.

Too sad.

DAY 92 24-JUNE-2020, MYSORE, INDIA

The tale of a broken chair

I don't know how to tell you. Well, I slipped and fell. Last night, the plastic chair I sat on collapsed and broke. I fell on the floor in a thud and hurt my back slightly. For the past 3 years, the chair was bathroom chair for my son, for taking bath, as he cannot walk due to peripheral neuropathy. Few days ago, I fell too. But the chair didn't break. The legs just bent and gave away.

I must buy a new one as soon as possible tomorrow. Otherwise it will be problem for bath for my son.

Today, after the incident, I feel strange that I had to fall without me knowing. It was sudden and I couldn't support myself.

My life is broken too. Like the chair I fell along and broke.

I just don't know how to fix it.

Do I have time?

DAY 96 28-JUNE-2020, MYSORE, INDIA

Pandemic Again

"Take whatever precautions we can, rest is left to our fate"

"True but sad."

Corona virus cases are rising fast in the state.

The last two major pandemics in India - Plague in 1890s and Spanish Flu in 1918s were under Britishers. The deaths were in millions, as Britishers let the disease spread in India during the initial stages. We have our own Indian government now; we didn't let the disease spread in the beginning early March. Now the corona virus will spread through our society as lockdowns are unlocked, but with all the preparedness the deaths will be minimized. That the society will face the wrath is for sure, mainly spread through people living in close quarters. We all need to be alert and maintain the precautions. The long-term scars will remain, though.

Like every pandemic carries its lessons.

I SEE YOU

The mangoes spread in front of the 85-year old man,

three varieties of mangoes, placed in red, blue, black trays;

he looked motionless, as I drove past,

masked, breathing hot air onto my glasses.

I see you. I see you go towards Metagalli, after an hour,

Sit motionless on gravel, mangoes in their trays,

until I come to buy, two kilos of banganapalli variety,

then you talk, all the void in eternity,

until I talk too, I hear you,

until I talk again, I hear you,

one final time, until I take out one hundred rupee note

a small token of my contribution, unburdening

what I have pent up for the past two months

O old man! I see you, O depressed man! I see you.

CHINESE KILLS

The beautiful Eastern Ladakh's Galwan valley stands mute witness

barbarism, like centuries ago, animal behavior short of

humans eat human, kill, kill, clubs, nails, logs with nails, rods,

tainted, stabbed in the back, traitor lurking in the dark,

like a thief out to steal other's property; here we have China kill,

worse than barbaric, ungentlemanly, no remorse ever.

I have started to hate Chinese. I normally don't hate anyone.

Now Chinese, only, thinking whole night, browsing websites,

how did we get into this? How did we let it upon us?

Three things torturing my mind – Corona virus, lockdown with loss of jobs,

and China kill-kill, erasing any saner thoughts we ever had.

My great Himalayas, my dear 73-year old country, soaked

in religious hymns, pujas for salvaging, blood.

O Galwan river soaked red! O dead bodies floating!

VIKAS DUBEY 10.07.2020

In the annals of pandemic 2019-20, there remains etched a violent criminal going by – Vikas Dubey. He killed impudently, more policemen. Looks like nobody fears policemen anymore. He was contemplating, how to dispose off the dead policemen bodies – burn them? bury them? Then he got the signal to run, run for his life. More policemen were coming to his door. He made his own arrangements to counterattack. 8 more policemen lost their lives. Police became fodder for his mafia activities. Uttar Pradesh is the state, where mafia and police live… both friends and foes.

There is this corona virus pandemic, there is this criminal intent. One is unseen, the other one happens right before us, a.k.a. Bollywood crime thriller. Both news grabs the headlines. Crime in the morning, Corona virus cases and deaths by evening, when the counts get released.

And then there is me. Yes me. I just lost my job, almost. My manager forced me to put in my papers with 90-day notice. Life's turning circles and cycles. Life's isn't ocean to swim around in dinghies.

19-JULY-2020, MYSORE, INDIA

The World Around Us

5.30 am.

I couldn't sleep much in the night. Woke up at 5am. There are so many things I wanted to do. Lost my job, almost. Serving notice period. Searching for jobs, both as a freelancer or full time. Whichever comes first. Almost like, first come, first served. Sometimes I feel that I can set up a Medical School. Need acres of land though. Who will pay? I have the capability of setting up a world-class institution. Seriously, I am contemplating buying land near Maddur for the Medical School. Perhaps I want to change the way students and Indian population understand why health matters, and how the institution can change the mindset of all – maintain health forever.

Outside the entire street is barricaded by rigid frame barriers, thorny plants, deprecated tables, boulders – anything to prevent people from moving out. Fortunately, someone created an opening for a single person to slide through. These are not normal times. The house across has a corona virus positive patient. She has been shifted to Covid center at Akash Medical Hospital. One patient is enough, for the entire street to be quarantined into a red zone. There is a weighty responsibility on all of us, not to be a carrier. Break the chain is the mantra. And Bangalore is trying hard at it.

I am a deeply religious person, but I don't allow religion to rule my day. I am not like someone, who would sit Infront of the God and pray for hours at a stretch. The world needs to be silent during the time. People would talk in whispers. It is a new order, all in the name of Gods, Goddesses, and boobs to receive. I believe in Karma, and the inner calling. Take whatever comes in the way. It is Godsend. What we direct to do is our action. Both need to be in tandem. In it lies the future.

The truth is pandemic is on, in full swing. Even, right across the house. Then, I am working from home. Lost my job, almost. Looking for the next thoughts to take me till my death. Six years to retire (remember fifty-eight is retirement age), years to live.

All if I am not washed away by the corona virus pandemic.

JOB LOSS

This lockdown started on a negative note for me. I almost lost my job. My company put me on bench, as I exited a project just before lockdown started. More than job loss, there is a fear of revulsion at home, having lost a job. My family is more oriented towards having a salaried job, than an entrepreneur type. My wife would look at me, as I have suddenly become worthless. The initial few days of lockdown was of fear and uncertainty. If I were to lose my job, what would happen? Slowly it dawned that at least there is a Government directive not to let go employees, and my company is strict follower of Government directives. I was safe for few days or until lockdown holds. I would let myself think about how my life has been shaped. As I remember, I have always been a failure. The decisions I took has been proved wrong later in my life. The lockdown has revealed to my inner self, what wrongs I have done. Where I could have taken different decisions. I am at peace with myself, trying to refocus on the right things for my life. I need to be more vocal, be plain speaking, soft, yet subtle, and at times, funny. What matters is the ending. Whether it is the last visible face, last discussions, last smiles, or even the last time we ever did anything, including death. I am calm, slow, unwilling to rush through decisions. There is always time for everything, only thing was we never gave time for anything. We rushed through all along. Time to look at who we are, what are we up to, and how.

57

23-JULY-2020, BENGALURU, INDIA

I am Unwell

I am unwell for the past 10 days, with urine tract infection. Even the urine flow has reduced. Then I consulted my favorite doctor, who has saved me several times earlier. When the results of the tests came, there was nothing but shock and awe. Is the results me?

I never imagined in my life, that my blood sugar count would rise so significantly, and that there will be two sort of infection – Yeast and Enterococcus Faecalis. Doctor put me into Blood Sugar tablets, and antibiotics. Yesterday, my stomach was bloated like a balloon.

One of my seniors at work, enquired if this was Covid? "I don't think so," I told him.

Coming to Corona virus, the cases in Bangalore is touching 2000+ marks for the past several days and the stage rising to 5000+ positive cases. Time is coming for the city to be swept by the deadly contagious virus.

GOING, GOING, AND MORE GOING AND GONE

A giggle over numbers, of positives, and deaths
led to positive notes. Well done, government,

by the bigger government – like father and son
praising each other to the hilt. Well done, well done!

People praised and appreciated. Karnataka has done it
Flattened the curve compared to rest of India. Don't look
our way!

While New Delhi and Mumbai rose in record numbers.
Don't look our way, we are happy with our numbers.

Then the difference was seen, when I thought of an
inter-district travel. To see aged folks in the family.

Mysuru to Bengaluru travel by car. I told of safety,
not to open the windows, no breathing of any

who am I to judge others, other behavior, breathing onto us,

those bike riders, cyclists, walking without masks on.

I read in an article, to assume, everyone around

are corona virus carriers. Let me not be the judge.

We were riding, into rising numbers in Bengaluru, day-by day.

Soon the opposite house had a corona virus patient.

The cases rose four to five times, as my street was bound

on either side, with barricades, reflecting a red containment zone.

People tend to see different side of rising cases, like a falling

stock market - quit the city, go away. Some lumping

luggage's on carts, dumping themselves far,

away from Bengaluru. There are no guilty men and women.

They are simply running for their lives.
Who wants to be infected? Gone far away.

Going, going, going,
and more going and gone. I remain.

IDLI BATTER

The sound was disturbing, at a distance, like a calling.

I was in deep sleep, yet awakened to the sound, eyes closed,

Rolling on the bed in the wee hours

Around 3am. I found the machine is running.

We are all idli type, soft, yet healthy – what we eat for

Breakfast, sets the tone of the day – we eat our day.

It is the taste of a lifetime. My mother-in-law will make.

It is the same, never different. Like a recipe passed

Down generations. But the generation started with her.

The sound still disturbing, the lights on in the room. I was

Decided to wake up, one step at a time, I stepped down,

Wiping my eyes, lest I slip and fall, tried to stop

The method to madness we all see. Shouts, angers, abuses

For all things tasteless. Some throw the breakfast plate

To a madness I couldn't fathom.

Men shout, women quiver, trying to wash away

The sins, as if they want the world to be just that,

Be the same, irrespective

As if they knew man versus woman, son versus daughter,

As if they knew only son's matter.

THE YEAR OF GOD

A year ended, a new year started, like a chain
like always, new year's a celebration
of success and failures, of what we look to relook
at the countdown. I found Wuhan more interesting.
Something is happening in China, we'd make fun
of, it never happens in India, are we in control?
There's this new virus, named Covid-19.
We move to 2020. Fun notwithstanding.
We are all in control, the world smiled,
as Chinese died, inside and outside
hospitals. Many ran helter-skelter.
This time, to countries around the world,
fearful and feverish, carried
the virus out of their natives to the new native.
The new year dawned to deaths and loss of life
Like never, in a way out of control,
Drawn by an invisible force. Like God.
Those who laughed at the fever flu, forgot
Their words would bite back, they died too,
As if the God saw them, justice to deliver.

RE-LOCKDOWN

I wonder if I had grown up with lockdowns as a term,

to know what it really is like, been there done that type,

sure of what it is, and how to shutter myself in, boxed
over:

the world outside not to be seen, except for essentials,

for all that we grown up with, freedom to move, think,

peruse the mindless people walking as if they are on top

of each other. Then came first of the many lockdowns,

have spent talking about it, soon the topics changed,

loneliness set in, I needed to talk in person, talking

was never enough if I met anyone, vegetable vendors,

supermarket tellers, I suppose I am talking to all,

each wall around me, facing a sudden drop in me.

LIFE IS LIKE THAT

The world around us has no limits,
no likes, no dislikes, all abstract,
like the one we face, evert day, fits
our virus gap – called Corona.

I looked at the data, since the lockdown
days, and what do I see? New and more
positives, Bollywood heroes, felling down
ministers, and MLAs, rushing to the fore.

The best hospitals have lined up packages,
to turn the grief into a happy ending,
from bed to service, from healing since ages,
boosting immunity, pills, powders, and teas.

The music of the pandemic is reaching
crescendo, as more and more wickets
are falling. You see them sad with words,
rushing to get admitted, search for beds.

Life is like that. We run and run, when

we want something urgent, desperate,

instead of plan and treat, instead hurried,

uncertain, and cloudy: life is like that only.

LIFE AND BED

I wonder if there was anytime humanity ever existed here,

man eats man, dog eats dog, no likes, no dislikes, all abstract, aka corona virus.

I did notice the rising positive cases and deaths taking people.

I have spent time at the covid hospital, tending to an injured. I see people wait for

something or other, some wait for beds, some wait to see them,

near one's death, property and money, tears, and joys for some;

the mind is all chaos; then some have abusive wife, even on hospital bed,

caring for, god only knows, the purpose.

What do we notice?

Nothing.

There's an empty space

We all try to fit in

For our selfish needs.

We want everything.

What we get is vacuum,

God lives by

Teaching us, how to live.

MASKED

Every birthday, we age, the younger

we tend to behave.

Look around. What do you see?

You see everyone and yourself. You see others in you.

Closeted with no opening. You see the God next you,

look at you, smile, nod, wave hand to assure.

I waited hours, days, months, and years

like this morning, taking the glance in, all ears,

I had noticed the power, silent, yet forceful, guide me,

as I tread, goading me more towards my goals.

Outside is silent, and fearful. The lockdown kept everyone

inside their homes, fearing to catch the unknown virus.

It needs your presence, in us, with us. The world is
masked.

So am I, careful not to inhale or exhale the virus?

The humanity, out there, too honest to see the virus guile
—

alert but careless. O God, I am aging.

I want to age more and not cut short.
I do want a return trip and seek your

blessings. Not once, not twice, I hesitate to seek answers
to my thoughts, giving away, like waves in ocean split
open,

as Lord Rama walked.
We seek to sail through.

VAGABOND

the semi naked beggar
who tapped on the windows
of cars stopping or slowing
at the traffic signal
I always saw

him to limp fast
at the cars and people
on the two-wheelers
walk away dejected
every day I saw

the frail skeleton
until covid struck the town
people falling like pins
this man too, dies
on the road side

poor soul

lay on the grass

until the city workers

cloaked in covid kits

left in me sorry tears.

HARI COURTED DEATH

I

You made delicious menu for breakfast

During covid lockdowns

And you promised to come

After the lockdown was lifted

And we spoke several times after

Not knowing you were seriously ill

For several days, almost bed ridden

With rising fever, chills, cough

Even you didn't want to see a doctor

Why? You feared they will take you away

And quarantine you in some hospital

You feared a secret unknown death.

When the municipal folks came over

You asked them to go away

And shouted at them, shooed them away

Not one relative came for help, feared too

The faith to help was missing

My heart bled when I heard you left

This abode of mortals, silent, helpless

I wept, wept every time I thought of you

And I was always thinking of you.

I didn't realize you courted death

She was your bride, you were her man

You remained a bachelor until death,

As if death waited for you with her arms

Wide enough to hug you, and you waded

Right into her arms, married finally

While we fellow mortals watched

You became immortal, a silent star.

11

I always wanted your call. You were your chirpy self.

And you knew your finances, how, and where to lend.
You would take your Vespa all over the town

Painting the words lend, cash, and interest.

But due to covid situation, I feared you'd catch it

From some passive or active carriers

Sick you became, soon looking to self-medicate
With the cold, and fever tablets.

Your words sound worrisome, non-stop, high fever,
Refusing to subside – even your voice went hoarse.
When we gave the doctor details, you brushed off
Saying all doctors are useless-well, sort of quacks.

Then what? You stopped picking calls, too many calls
Ignoring the help and advice offered to you
Our worried calls. Your mother didn't lift either.
Then came the dreaded call-you were too sick

Lift off the bed. Not corona, everyone would say
Not corona. Just some cold, and chest infection.
We believed too. Not corona. Not anymore.
But we forgot you could die soon, silent, unknown.

THE SILENT WARRIORS

I never doubted your capacity to cure the nation of its ills

And this virus is imported too – for we know little

The comforting factor is the known symptom

And deceptive too, for we stay relaxed.

While it eats us from within.

The cure lies in the healing.

The soft touch that soothes, allowing

A fightback against the deadly sting inside.

The turmoil in the world, as people die

Or get ready for the gunny bag of bodies

There remain the lone warriors without

Their usual arms, without vaccine or cure.

I wish we have what it takes

We have the warriors, we need the cure

Little known warriors fought to save each life,

As I see it, they died too, among the counted.

IN MEMORIUM BELAGUR BINDU MADHAVA SWAMIJI

27-Nov-2020

I never thought you would also take a hit.

You are the living god

And you are the Hanuman.

Today I got a jolt, like electric shock

Of my life, looking at the message,

That you were no more, died of corona virus.

The inside of my body became cloudy,

And it rained through my eyes.

Even downpours seem little,

As the day passed, overflowing in tears.

There's nothing I could do, except

Remind myself of-your

Blessings.

Silent prayers ring aloud, awaiting your vision,

My lips tremble, my chin hurts of weeping.

I thought the world would move on,

Lingering thoughts.

But there is the world didn't wait to

Rush to your wrapped body,

Surrounded by PPE people, reminding

How fast people can become immortal.

DEJA VU – COVID REVISITED

It's all over again.

Everyone did what they lacked –

    Community – a world revisited,

No masks evident, no distance,

    Carefree – we are not ourselves.

I've been patient so long.

And without knowing we see –

    Deja vu – Omicron – a virus revisited.

An imagined lockdown again

    Déjà vu – empty streets – and fear again.

Never think beyond the obvious.

Infections, hospitalizations,

    More of it – ten times or at least

Rewoven into our mind

    A sense of fear, tapestries – of spikes.

I CAN'T BREATHE

April is supposed to be when flowers bloom, color our vision, into welcoming harsher weathers as the year rolls by. This April, the air got tinted red. The corona virus rose like a phoenix, more matured, complex mutation, with ability to cause havoc. And it did. The effect was almost instant, with people rushing to breath, oxygen levels plummeting. Oxygen cylinders running out, hospital lacking beds. The scene was set right, to explode – both cases and deaths. Individual families were frantic, searching for oxygen cylinders, ICU beds, even spreading through Whatsapp, Twitter, in the hope someone will come forward and help.

India is crying for help.

India is crying.

The world around is collapsing, like a pack of cards blown by wind.

I am scared to go out. I am not a fearful person. But I don't want to die a dog's death, where people run away from the dead body, and someone does the cremation rites without a sense of respect.

People are dying dog's death. On the streets, in their cars, on pavements, on hospital corridors, in their homes.

Suddenly life has become fearful – of the unknown.

www.ingramcontent.com/pod-product-compliance
Lightning Source LLC
Chambersburg PA
CBHW021338160726
47994CB00007B/2752